MW01014919

2018-2019

The Job Hunting Handbook

by Harry Dahlstrom

The Job Hunting Handbook

Copyright © 2018 2019 by Harry Dahlstrom
ALL RIGHTS RESERVED
No part of this book may be reproduced

PHOTOCOPYING OR ELECTRONIC SCANNING OF THIS
DOCUMENT IS UNLAWFUL AND EXPRESSLY PROHIBITED

ISBN 978-0-940712-23-2
Printed in the United States of America

Published by
Dahlstrom & Company, Inc.
50 October Hill Road
Holliston, MA 01746
Tel: 1-800-222-0009
www.DahlstromCo.com

Cover photography
Shutterstock
Copyright, Arthimedes

Design
ChrisHerronDesign.com

Special thanks
Deb Holmes, Ann Keenan, Jamie Dahlstrom, Gail Dahlstrom,
Chris Herron, Susan Plawsky, Andy Peterson, Lindsay
Dahlstrom, and the office pooch Scout

Free job-hunting tools and the latest national hiring trends at
www.HarryDahlstrom.com

Contents

Welcome to the American job market

The American job market is one of the most exciting marketplaces in the world. It's a place where millions of people compete for work. It's a place where careers are launched, where fortunes can be made, and where dreams can come true.

"My big dream is simply to get a good job."

And 2018-19 look to be good years for you to find that good job.

Q. "But, are employers hiring for my occupation too?"

Flip to page 6 and you'll see the Wages and Demand chart for the largest 175 occupations in the United States. Notice the occupational openings for your job. That's the number of yearly job opening, in thousands of jobs, for your occupation.

Q. "Then, let me ask you this—I filled-out dozens of job applications in the past month and not one employer has contacted me. What's going on?"

Competition.

There are 4 million unemployed people who are looking for jobs. Plus, there are millions of workers who have been waiting for the economy to improve so they could change jobs. They're jumping into the job market too.

You are competing with lots of job hunters. Some employers are getting over 100 job applications for every job opening they post.

Annual hires, in millions of people

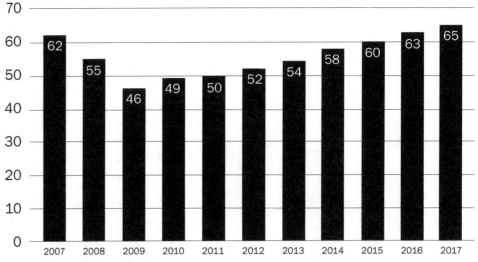

Source: Bureau of Labor Statistics

Q. "How can I compete with all those people?"

Don't let the numbers scare you. Most job hunters are not very organized and most don't know how to look for a job. They're just winging it.

Too many people think job hunting means sitting in front of a computer, reading help-wanted ads, filling out job-applications, crossing their fingers for good luck, and waiting for an employer to call. Sadly, with so many people competing for each job, their phones never ring.

Q. "What should I do?"

This is important—employers are always looking for *good* people. Even during the worst part of the recession, when employers stopped hiring, it's amazing how quickly a hiring freeze would thaw when right person started chipping away at the ice.

To help you become that right person, you'll need to know how employers hire so you can outsmart the competition. You'll need to know what employers really want so you can offer them the help they truly need. And, you'll need to know how to sell yourself so the employer can spot you—and hire you—instead of someone else.

You can do this. It's easy. Everything you need is right here in 48 pages. Plus, you can read the whole thing in an hour or so and get started today.

Q. "Show me."

Okay. Turn to page 8 and let's see how employers hire new people.

FIRST THINGS FIRST

Before we get started, if you're new to the job market or if you're thinking about switching to a different line of work, you need to choose a specific occupation.

If you apply for a job without naming a specific occupation, some employers will put you where they need you. This means you'll run the risk of getting stuck in a job you'll hate, stuck in a dead-end job with no chance for advancement, or stuck in a job with frequent layoffs and no job security. Don't let some stranger decide your future. Take charge of your life and choose your own occupation.

Here are six easy ways to choose an occupation:

· Start with your wish list. What kind of work have you always dreamed of doing?

· Think about your friends and relatives. Do you know people who have the kind of jobs you'd like to have?

· Think about the things you love to do. Do you have a hobby or a passion that you could turn into an occupation?

· Think about your talents. Do you have a special talent, skill, or ability that could be turned into an occupation?

· Try a career test. Log onto a computer and Google "career tests." Career tests analyze your personality by asking a few dozen multiple-choice questions. Then, they match your personality to occupations you'd be good at. Give it a try. You might be surprised at what they recommend. Most tests are free, so try several different tests. Caution—use the test results only as a guide, not a rule. No test is totally accurate.

· Need some help choosing an occupation? Contact a career counselor at your school or your local American Job Center. Career counselors will not choose a career for you. But, they could administer some special aptitude tests and help you explore some options. To find a job center near you, Google, American Job Centers or One Stop Career Centers

© COPYRIGHT, HARRY DAHLSTROM

Wages & Demand For The 175 Largest U.S. Occupations Through 2026

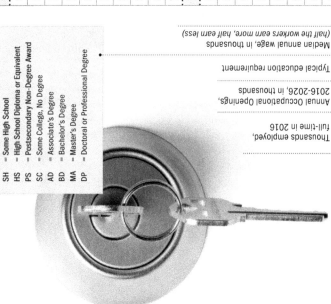

Education & Training Codes

- SH = Some High School
- HS = High School Diploma or Equivalent
- PS = Postsecondary Non-Degree Award
- SC = Some College, No Degree
- AD = Associate's Degree
- BD = Bachelor's Degree
- MA = Master's Degree
- DP = Doctoral or Professional Degree

Column key:
- Thousands employed, full-time in 2016
- Annual Occupational Openings, 2016-2026, in thousands
- Typical education requirement
- Median annual wage, in thousands (half the workers earn more, half earn less)

Occupation	Employed (000s)	Openings (000s)	Education	Median Wage (000s)
Roofers	146.2	16.6	SH	$38

Education, Training & Library Occupations

Occupation	Employed (000s)	Openings (000s)	Education	Median Wage (000s)
Elementary School Teachers	1,410.9	112.8	BD	$56
Kindergarten Teachers	154.4	16.7	BD	$53
Librarians	138.2	14.5	MA	$58
Middle School Teachers	630.3	50.5	BD	$57
Postsecondary Teachers	1,871.4	172.4	PHD	$67
Preschool Teachers	478.5	53.6	AD	$29
Secondary School Teachers	1,018.7	79.5	BD	$58
Self-Enrichment Education Teachers	354.2	46.3	HS	$37
Special Education Teachers	480.6	38.5	BD	$58
Teacher Assistants	1,308.1	147.9	HS	$25

Food Preparation & Serving Occupations

Occupation	Employed (000s)	Openings (000s)	Education	Median Wage (000s)
Bartenders	611.2	102.3	SH	$21
Bussers & Barbacks	3,452.2	736	SH	$19
Combined Food Prep & Servers	517.6	67.2	SH	$20
Cooks, Fast Food	424.8	64.4	SH	$25
Cooks, Institution & Cafeteria	1,231.9	195.3	SH	$24
Cooks, Restaurant	185.9	24.7	SH	$22
Cooks, Short Order	505.2	113.2	SH	$20
Counter Attendants	431.2	78.2	SH	$20
Dishwashers	514.3	83	SH	$21
Food Preparation Workers	871.1	157.7	SH	$21
Hosts & Hostesses	409.2	97.9	SH	$20
Waiters & Waitresses	2,600.5	522.7	SH	$20

Healthcare Practitioners & Technical Occupations

Occupation	Employed (000s)	Openings (000s)	Education	Median Wage (000s)
Dental Hygienists	207.9	17.5	AD	$73
EMTs & Paramedics	248	19.3	PS	$33
Licensed Practical & Vocational Nurses	724.5	62.7	PS	$44
Medical & Clinical Lab Technicians	164.2	12.9	AD	$39
Medical & Clinical Lab Technologists	171.4	12.9	BD	$61
Medical Records Technicians	206.3	15.8	PS	$38
Pharmacists	312.5	15.3	PHD	$122
Pharmacy Technicians	402.5	37.5	HS	$31

Occupation	Employed (000s)	Openings (000s)	Education	Median Wage (000s)
Medical & Health Services Managers	352.2	36.4	BD	$97
Property Managers	317.3	28.4	HS	$57
Sales Managers	385.5	36.2	BD	$118
Social & Community Service Managers	147.3	15.8	BD	$65

Office & Administrative Support Occupations

Occupation	Employed (000s)	Openings (000s)	Education	Median Wage (000s)
Bill & Account Collectors	305.7	30.2	HS	$35
Billing & Posting Clerks	501	59.6	HS	$36
Bookkeeping & Accounting Clerks	1,730.5	186.6	HS	$38
Customer Service Representatives	2,784.5	373.4	HS	$32
Data Entry Keyers	203.8	16.8	HS	$30
Dispatchers	201.7	18	HS	$38
Executive Secretaries & Assistants	685.3	54.6	HS	$56
File Clerks	135	14.2	HS	$29
Hotel, Motel & Resort Desk Clerks	252.6	40.9	HS	$22
Human Resources Assistants	141.5	15.1	HS	$39
Insurance Claims & Policy Clerks	308.5	35.6	HS	$38
Legal Secretaries	194.7	15	HS	$44
Loan Interviewers & Clerks	229.8	25.7	HS	$39
Medical Secretaries	574.2	80.8	HS	$34
Office Clerks, General	3,117.7	356.2	HS	$31
Payroll & Timekeeping Clerks	166.3	16.1	HS	$42
Postal Service Mail Carriers	316.7	16.1	HS	$58
Receptionists & Information Clerks	1,063.7	151.2	HS	$28
Secretaries & Administrative Assistants	2,536.2	244.3	HS	$35
Shipping, Receiving & Traffic Clerks	681.4	67.2	HS	$31
Stock Clerks & Order Fillers	2,008.6	269.3	HS	$24
Tellers	502.7	51.5	HS	$27

Personal Care & Service Occupations

Occupation	Employed (000s)	Openings (000s)	Education	Median Wage (000s)
Amusement & Recreation Attendants	300	73.2	SH	$20
Childcare Workers	1,216.6	188.8	HS	$21
Fitness Trainers & Aerobics Instructors	299.2	54.8	HS	$38
Hairdressers & Cosmetologists	617.3	82.4	PS	$24
Nonfarm Animal Caretakers	241.5	45.2	SH	$22
Recreation Workers	390	70.6	BD	$24

Architecture & Engineering Occupations

Occupation	Employed (000s)	Openings (000s)	Education	Median Wage (000s)
Civil Engineers	303.5	25.9	BD	$84
Electrical Engineers	188.3	13.9	BD	$94
Industrial Engineers	257.9	19.7	BD	$84
Mechanical Engineers	288.8	21.2	BD	$84

Arts, Design, Entertainment, Sports & Media Occupations

Occupation	Employed (000s)	Openings (000s)	Education	Median Wage (000s)
Actors	63.8	7.4	SC	$0
Coaches & Scouts	276.1	42	HS	$31
Graphic Designers	266.3	26.2	BD	$48
Musicians & Singers	172.4	18	HS	$0
Photographers	147.3	9.7	HS	$34
Public Relations Specialist	259.6	28.3	BD	$58
Writers & Authors	131.2	12.7	BD	$61

Occupation				
Landscapers & Groundskeepers	1,197.9	161.1	SH	$26
Maids & Housekeeping Cleaners	1,443.2	200.8	SH	$22
Business & Financial Operations Occupations				
Accountants & Auditors	1,397.7	141.8	BD	$68
Claims Adjusters, Examiners & Investigators	311.1	24.5	HS	$64
Compliance Officers	288.3	25.9	BD	$67
Financial Analysts	296.1	29	BD	$82
Loan Officers	318.6	30.5	HS	$64
Management Analysts	806.4	81.3	BD	$81
Market Research Analysts	595.4	76.7	BD	$63
Personal Financial Advisors	271.9	25.4	BD	$91
Purchasing Agents	309.4	23.8	HS	$63
Community & Social Service Occupations				
Child, Family & School Social Workers	317.6	37.9	BD	$43
Clergy	243.9	29.2	BD	$46
Guidance & Vocational Counselors	291.7	34.8	MA	$55
Healthcare Social Workers	176.5	22.5	MA	$54
Mental Health Counselors	157.7	20.8	MA	$43
Rehabilitation Counselors	119.3	13.9	MA	$35
Social & Human Service Assistants	389.8	55.4	HS	$32
Computer & Mathematical Occupations				
Computer Programmers	294.9	15.4	BD	$80
Computer Support Specialists	835.3	71.8	SC	$52
Computer Systems Analysts	600.5	44.8	BD	$87
Network & Computer Systems Admins	391.3	27	BD	$80
Software Developers, Applications	831.3	85.5	BD	$100
Software Developers, System Software	425	32.7	BD	$107
Web Developers	162.9	14.2	AD	$66
Construction & Extraction Occupations				
Carpenters	1,025.6	104.9	HS	$44
Cement Masons & Concrete Finishers	178.9	22.4	SH	$39
Construction Laborers	1,216.7	145.7	SH	$33
Electricians	666.9	82.1	HS	$53
Operating Engineers	371.1	47.3	HS	$46
Painters, Construction & Maintenance	381.5	35.4	SH	$38
Plumbers, Pipefitters & Steamfitters	480.6	61.1	HS	$51

Occupation				
Radiologic Technologists	205.2	13.6	AD	$57
Registered Nurses	2,955.2	203.6	AD	$68
Veterinarians	79.6	4.5	PHD	$89
Healthcare Support Occupations				
Dental Assistants	332	45.9	PS	$37
Home Health Aides	911.5	167.7	SH	$23
Massage Therapists	160.3	21.9	PS	$40
Medical Assistants	634.4	95	HS	$32
Nursing Assistants	1,510.3	193.6	PS	$25
Installation, Maintenance & Repair Occupations				
Automotive Body & Related Repairers	160.4	17.2	HS	$42
Automotive Technicians & Mechanics	749.9	75.9	HS	$38
Bus & Truck Mechanics	278.8	28.3	HS	$45
HVAC&R Mechanics & Installers	332.9	38.7	PS	$46
Industrial Machinery Mechanics	346.9	33	HS	$50
Maintenance & Repair Workers	1,432.6	154.7	HS	$37
Telecom Equipment Installers & Repairers	237.6	21.9	PS	$54
Telecom Line Installers & Repairers	106.1	10.7	HS	$53
Legal Occupations				
Judges & Magistrates	28.4	1.4	PHD	$126
Lawyers	792.5	41.9	PHD	$118
Paralegals & Legal Assistants	285.6	34.7	AD	$50
Management Occupations				
Administrative Services Managers	281.7	26.2	HS	$90
Architectural & Engineering Managers	180.1	13.6	BD	$135
Chief Executives	308.9	20.1	BD	$181
Computer & Info. Systems Managers	367.6	32.5	BD	$136
Construction Managers	403.8	33.4	AD	$89
Education Administrators, K-12	251.3	21.2	MA	$93
Education Administrators, Postsecondary	180.1	15.7	MA	$91
Farm, Ranch & Agricultural Managers	1,028.7	84.8	HS	$66
Financial Managers	580.4	56.8	BD	$122
Food Service Managers	308.7	36.7	HS	$51
General & Operations Managers	2,263.1	210.8	BD	$99
Industrial Production Managers	170.6	11.7	AD	$97
Marketing Managers	218.3	21.3	BD	$131

Occupation				
Electrical Equipment Assemblers	218.9	18.2	HS	$31
Helpers, Production Workers	426	72	SH	$25
Inspectors, Testers, Sorters & Weighers	520.7	52.7	HS	$37
Laundry & Dry-Cleaning Workers	220.1	29.4	SH	$22
Machinists	396.2	40.8	HS	$42
Meat, Poultry & Fish Cutters & Trimmers	156.4	19.1	SH	$24
Packaging & Filling Machine Operators	383	44.6	HS	$28
Printing Press Operators	178.7	16	HS	$36
Team Assemblers	1,130.9	107.7	HS	$30
Welders, Cutters, Solderers & Brazers	404.8	45.8	HS	$39
Protective Services Occupations				
Correctional Officers & Jailers	450	31.3	HS	$43
Firefighters	327.3	24.3	PS	$48
Police & Sheriff's Patrol Officers	684.2	49.5	HS	$60
Security Guards	1,123.3	157.5	HS	$26
Sales & Related Occupations				
Cashiers	3,555.5	653.9	SH	$20
Counter & Rental Clerks	458.2	61.8	SH	$26
Insurance Sales Agents	501.4	54.5	HS	$50
Parts Salespersons	251.9	32.9	SH	$30
Real Estate Sales Agents	348.8	34.6	SH	$44
Retail Salespersons	4,602.5	671.7	SH	$23
Sales Reps, Wholesale & Manufacturing	1,469.9	159.1	HS	$57
Securities & Financial Sales Agents	375.7	38	BD	$67
Telemarketers	216.6	33.3	SH	$24
Transportation & Material Moving Occupations				
Bus Drivers, School or Special Client	507.9	64.8	HS	$30
Bus Drivers, Transit & Intercity	179.3	23.9	HS	$40
Driver/Sales Workers	467.9	48.4	HS	$23
Heavy & Tractor-Trailer Truck Drivers	1,871.7	214.3	HS	$41
Industrial Truck & Tractor Operators	549.9	65.9	SH	$32
Laborers & Material Movers, Hand	2,628.4	388.6	SH	$26
Light Truck or Delivery Drivers	953.5	110.2	HS	$31
Packers & Packagers, Hand	710.8	108.4	SH	$22
Refuse & Recyclable Material Collectors	136	18.9	SH	$35
Taxi Drivers & Chauffeurs	305.1	32.7	SH	$24

© COPYRIGHT, HARRY DAHLSTROM

How employers hire

Tom Turnover handed in his two-week notice. He's leaving the job. Helen Hiresmore jumps into action. She's the hiring manager. When Tom leaves, the department will be under-staffed. So, Helen needs to find someone to replace Tom. And that starts the hiring process.

The job description is reviewed

Helen begins by looking over the job description for Tom's position. Every job in her company has one.

The job description is a document that explains the important duties needed to perform the job. It becomes an important guide when writing help-wanted advertisements, reading resumes, screening job hunters, and conducting job interviews.

You might say that the job description is a yardstick. Anyone who applies for the job is measured against it.

The job opening is announced

Like most hiring managers, Helen starts by announcing the job opening to her employees.

Some employees might want the job. Other employees may have friends who would be a good fit for the opening—and Helen would like to talk with them.

If Helen needs to see additional resumes, she can post the job opening on the employment page of her company's web site. She can also post help-wanted advertisements with job banks and the media, attend job fairs, host an open house, and request resumes from career centers and employment agencies.

Resumes come pouring in

When a resume lands on Helen's desk, she'll give it a quick ten-second glance. See, when looking at a resume, Helen is primarily looking for the five or six important requirements listed in the job description. She can tell in a glance whether the resume has them or not.

If a resume has the "right stuff," she'll set it aside for a closer look. If it doesn't, a polite

55% of the labor force work for small businesses
26% of the labor force work for medium-size businesses
19% of the labor force work for large businesses

Small = under 100 employees, Medium = 100-499 employees, Large = 500 employees or more

—U.S. Census Bureau

rejection letter will be sent.

At large companies, resumes are downloaded into their computer's ATS, or Applicant Tracking Software.

The ATS actually reads every resume it receives—and it hunts for resumes that have the requirements listed in the job description. Resumes that have the right stuff are flagged and forwarded to the hiring manager for a closer look.

Sadly, sixty-five percent of all resumes do not have the right stuff and the ATS rejects them.

Phone calls are made

When Helen finds a resume with the right stuff, she'll phone the job hunter. This phone call is a screening call.

During the call, Helen will ask questions about the job hunter's experience and availability. If she thinks the person is a good fit for the job, he'll be invited to visit the company for a face-to-face job interview.

Interviews are scheduled

Helen wants to personally meet the five or six people who passed her telephone screens.

She wants to drill down into their skills and accomplishments. She wants to see how solid they are. She also wants to get a fix on their personalities. Like most hiring managers, Helen tries not to hire difficult people.

Of the five or six people interviewed for the job, two finalists usually stand out.

References are checked

Like eighty percent of all hiring managers, Helen will contact their references.

She will also contact their former schools and employers to verify their education and employment claims.

She will even visit their blogs, websites, Facebook, Linkedin, and Twitter sites to get a sense of their personalities and interests.

After evaluating the results, one person usually stands out.

The job is offered

Finally, Helen gets to make the phone call we all want to hear. "I would like to invite you join our team."

After the yahoos and screams of joy have subsided, wages, benefits, and a start date are discussed. Like many employers, Helen also requires that the new hire pass a medical examination and a background check.

And that's how Helen gets her employee.

Q. "But, suppose I don't have any work experience?"

Don't panic. In the next two chapters, you'll learn how to show that you do have the right stuff—even if you have no job experience.

Q. "How does anyone make it through this hiring gauntlet?"

It's easier than you might think.

In the following pages, we'll walk through the four cuts that managers use to weed out the weak job hunters. You'll learn: 1) How to create a resume that has all the "right stuff." 2) How to pass the telephone screen. 3) How to navigate through the five parts of a job interview. And, 4) how to find references who will sing your praises and help you win a job offer.

As you know, everything starts with the right stuff. So, turn the page and let's go find the right stuff for the job you want.

WHY THIS LONG DRAWN-OUT HIRING PROCESS?

There are two reasons, actually. Money and mistakes.

It's expansive to find the right person for the job. Did you know that it costs about $4,100 for a mid-size company to recruit and hire just one person?

It's also difficult to pick the right person. A Corporate Executive Board survey found that 20 percent of new hires are "regretted decisions." These are people who should not have been hired.

Twenty percent. That's two bad hires out of every ten people hired. It's also $7,400 in hiring costs. And that does not include the lost investment in wages, benefits, training, and productivity.

Hiring people is both expensive and risky. That's why the long hiring process.

© COPYRIGHT, HARRY DAHLSTROM

Show the employer that you have the "right stuff"

Every occupation has certain requirements. Carpenters must know how to read building plans. Sales people must know how to close a sale. Customer-service people must know how to work with difficult people. Managers must know how to motivate people to get the job done. What's the right stuff for your occupation? Don't guess. Find out. Show that you have the specific skills employers want. Here's how—

Let's take it from the beginning.

I'm sure you know what a portrait photographer does. So, let's use that occupation in the following example.

1. Name the job you want

> *Portrait photographer*

2. List the requirements of the job from the help-wanted advertisement

> *Capture the spirit of the subject*
> *Set up the equipment for the photo shoot*
> *Create the setting to get the best shot*
> *Position and coach the subject*
> *Schedule appointments to view photo proofs and sell photo packages*

3. Select the first requirement from your list

> *Capture the spirit of the subject*

4. Give an example of when or how you performed it

> *Interviewed subjects and showed photo-posing samples to help identify and capture the spirit of each subject*

5. Add a few details

> *Interviewed and photographed approximately 700 subjects and creatively captured the spirit of each person*

6. Repeat steps 3, 4, and 5 for each additional job requirement on your list

• •

"Lack of technical skills," is the number-one reason employers have trouble filling job openings

—Manpower

Q. "Where can I find the job requirements for my occupation?"

All you need to do is visit Indeed, Career-builder, and Monster. Then, read a dozen help-wanted advertisements for your occupation.

In each ad, look for a statement like, "The ideal candidate will be able to ..." or "Job duties include ...." That's where the hiring manager tells you exactly what she's looking for.

Now, pick out the 5 or 6 common job requirements that all of the ads seem to want. That's the stuff today's hiring managers are looking for. That's the stuff you want to include in your resume.

Q. "What kind of examples should I give?"

Think about the projects you worked on. Specifically, what was accomplished and the special role you played. That's where your best examples will come from.

If you have no experience with a certain skill, think about the projects you worked on in school, military, sports, volunteering, or in your life experiences. Use those experiences as substitute skills (see resume examples on pages 16, 17 and 18).

Q. "How much detail should I include?"

Mention the important facts. Keep it simple. Whenever possible, include numbers to describe the volume, size, money, time, effort, or result of what you did. Numbers impress people. They allow us to visualize what was accomplished.

Oh—don't get into the why or how of each project. That's the back-story. Save those interesting details for your job interview.

Now, you try it.

1. Name the job you want

_____

2. List the job requirements

a. _____

b. _____

c. _____

d. _____

e. _____

3. Select the first job requirement from your list above

_____

_____

4. Give an example of when or how you performed it

_____

_____

_____

5. Add details

_____

_____

_____

_____

_____

_____

Continued on the next page—

SUBSTITUTE SKILLS

If you don't have one of the needed job requirements, offer a substitute. A substitute shows that you have similar knowledge.

Similar knowledge shows that you can learn the requirement quicker than if you had no knowledge of the requirement.

For example, if you don't have the sales experience required for a given job, you might talk about your charitable fund-raising accomplishments instead. Fundraising is similar to selling.

If you don't have the interior decorating experience needed for a job, show pictures of the decorating projects you created in your own home.

If you don't have the public speaking experience needed for another job, talk about the PowerPoint presentations you created and presented in high school or college.

Reach into those other areas of your life to find those substitute skills—military, school, sports, volunteering, hobbies, and home projects.

© COPYRIGHT, HARRY DAHLSTROM

HERE ARE A FEW EXAMPLES FROM DIFFERENT OCCUPATIONS THAT YOU CAN USE TO HELP TURN YOUR PAST PROJECTS INTO THE "RIGHT STUFF"

Select a requirement
Make sandwiches

Give an example
Made custom sandwiches in a mobile deli

Add details
Made 100s of custom sandwiches during lunch-hour rush in a 2-person mobile deli

Select a requirement
Schedule appointments

Give an example
Scheduled appointments in a dental office

Add details
Scheduled appointments in a 3 dentist office serving 200 patients monthly

Select a requirement
Improve website quality and usability

Give an example
Re-wrote shopping-cart code to simplify customer experience

Add details
Re-wrote shopping-cart code that reduced customer abandoned orders by 8%

• •

Select a **2nd** requirement from your list on page 11

_____

_____

Give an example of when or how you performed it

_____

_____

Add details

_____

_____

_____

_____

Select a **3rd** requirement from your list

_____

_____

Give an example of when or how you performed it

_____

_____

Add details

_____

_____

_____

_____

Select a requirement
Supervise personnel

Give an example
Supervised tech support team

Add details
Supervised tech-support team of 7 people who resolved about 900 cases a month

Select a requirement
Train and coach

Give an example
Trained and coached a military squad

Add details
Trained and coached a military squad to provide life-saving emergency-medical treatment in combat: gunshot wounds, explosives, bone fractures, burns, more

Select a requirement
Assist with accounts payable and accounts receivable

Give an example
Assisted bookkeeper with AP and AR for a retail store

Add details
Assisted bookkeeper with AP and AR for a retail store with over 500 accounts and annual sales of $2 million.

• •

Select a 4th requirement from your list

_____

_____

Give an example of when or how you performed it

_____

_____

_____

Add details

_____

_____

_____

_____

_____

Select the 5th requirement from your list

_____

_____

Give an example of when or how you performed it

_____

_____

_____

Add details

_____

_____

_____

_____

_____

Congratulations!

You just turned the job requirements into your accomplishments. Accomplishments impress employers. They show that you are the kind of person who delivers results.

© COPYRIGHT, HARRY DAHLSTROM

Use the "right stuff" to build a powerful resume

Looking for a job? Then, you need a resume. Your resume is your calling card, your advertisement, your brochure, your flyer. It's a one-page handout that shows what a great catch you are.

Q. "What can I do with a resume?"

Mail it. Email it. Post it online. Ask friends to give it to their managers. Hand it out at job fairs. Give it to employment agencies.

The idea is to get it into the hands of as many hiring managers as you can. If a hiring manager likes what she sees in your resume, you could get invited to a job interview.

Q. "What if I'm not a good writer?"

That's okay. Writing your resume is easy. You completed all the heavy thinking in the last chapter. All that's left to do is type it up.

Q. "Is there some official format or design for a resume?"

No. There is no official format for writing your resume. You can set up your resume any way you like. Feel free to change, modify, expand, ignore, or simplify any of the following suggestions. But, most people do include the following topics in their resumes—

1. Your contact information

Tell employers who you are and where they can reach you.

At the top of the page, type your full name, mailing address, telephone number with area code, plus your text or email address.

2. Your goal

In one short sentence, tell what kind of work you want.

- "Seeking full-time position as a dragon slayer."

- If you have little or no experience, say that you are: "Seeking a full-time, entry-level position as a dragon slayer."

Seventy-five percent of hiring managers said they prefer a chronological resume that lists your most recent job first.

—Career Journal

3. Your education

Start with your most recent school or program.

- On the first line in this section, give the award, certification, or degree earned plus the date of the award. If you haven't graduated, simply give the number of credits earned toward the award (36 credits earned toward a BS degree in magic).

- On the second line, give the school's name and city/state address.

- On the third line, list any classes or activities you participated in that would help you in the job you want.

- Repeat for additional schools.

4a. Work experience

Start with your most recent employer.

- On the first line in this section, give your job title plus your beginning and ending dates of employment. If you are still employed there, give your starting date and the word "Present" to show that you still hold that job.

- On the next line, give the employer's name and city/state address.

- On the next few lines, list the five or six job requirements with examples from your past (see your notes on pages 11-13).

- Repeat for additional employers.

4b. No work experience

Instead of a "Work Experience" section, create a section titled, "Accomplishments."

- On the first line in this section, name one of the job requirements.

- Under that job requirement, offer some substitute examples from school, sports, volunteering, or other life projects to show what you achieved in that area (see Substitute Skills on page 11).

- Repeat for each additional job requirement.

5. Your skills list

Create a section called "Skills."

Then, simply list the names of any important tools, devices, programs, procedures, skills, licenses, and systems that you can operate or perform.

6. Additional information

Create a section called "Additional Information."

You don't have to include this section in your resume. It's optional. But, it is a great place to mention any special talents, skills, abilities or awards that might interest an employer.

• •

On the next few pages, you'll find three resumes that you can use to model your resume on.

Notice how simple and clean they look. Bold headings, short sentences, and plenty of white space help the requirements jump off the page. Plus, each job requirement is phrased as an accomplishment with an example of what the writer did and numbers to show the size of the projects.

Creating your easy-to-scan resume is even easier than you think. Just use the fill-in-the-blank worksheet on page 19.

WHY YOU NEED A SKILLS LIST IN YOUR RESUME

Having a skills section in your resume can be important. Many large employers download the resumes they receive into a database. A database is a computer file that can hold millions of resumes and job applications.

Databases are searchable. That means, if a hiring manager searches her database for "Final Cut" or "Avid" the computer will pull up only the resumes of people who have that film-editing software in their resumes.

So, if you want the hiring manager's computer to pull up your resume, help it find you by including the names of all the important tools, programs, and systems you can operate or perform.

© COPYRIGHT, HARRY DAHLSTROM

Here's a sample resume showing no work experience

James B. Jobless
1 Hereicome Highway, Ourtown, US 00000
Cell/Text: 111/222-3333   Email: jbj@SC68.com

GOAL

Seeking an entry-level position in retail sales at a hardware store

EDUCATION

High School Diploma, 06/2018

Hometown High School, Ourtown, US 00000

- Enjoyed classes in public speaking, math, shop, and computers

ACCOMPLISHMENTS

Although I have no prior experience in retail sales, I believe the following accomplishments show that I could learn the job quickly—

Math Skills

- Maintained 3-year "B" average in algebra and geometry
- Managed $1,000 investment that earned 4.2% APR

People Skills

- Played checkers most Sunday afternoons with seniors at a nursing home
- Formed study group with 4 people to boost grades in French

Product Knowledge

- Automotive: My father is a mechanic and we rebuilt my '99 Volvo including the engine, brakes, and suspension
- Electronics: Programmed family's TV, BlueRay, and Cable Box to run on one remote
- Construction: Helped my aunt rebuild a 100 sq/ft screened-in porch on her home.

Selling

- Sold my '99 Volvo and earned a $120 profit
- Sold magazines door-to-door for charity, raised $300

ADDITIONAL INFORMATION

- Reliable—Missed only two days of school this year
- Honest—Returned $20 check-cashing error to my bank

Here's a sample resume showing only classroom experience

Lindsay U. Needajob
2 Icandoit Drive, Ourtown, US 00000
Cell/Text: 111/222-3333

GOAL
Seeking a full-time position in public relations with a non-profit organization

EDUCATION
BS in Communications, 06/2018
Beatrice Hart College, Ourtown, US 00000
- Enjoyed classes in Sociology, Journalism, Economics

ACCOMPLISHMENTS

Writing Skills
- Wrote 2,000 word feature story on, "How to Buy a Good Used Car"
- Wrote 500 word short piece on, "Why Lottery Winners Go Bankrupt After Winning Millions Of Dollars"

Public Speaking
- Presented a 10-point technical talk on how to "Recover Data after Your Hard Drive Crashes"
- Appeared in a 30-minute, on-campus TV talk-show, "How to Live on the Money You Have"

Research
- Polled 86 licensed drivers on, "Why People Throw Trash out of Their Car Windows While Driving."
- Analyzed survey data on, "Will There be a Good Job for Me After Graduation?"

Press Relations
- Persuaded local newspaper editor to join a symposium on, "Who's Writing the Rules of Grammar for Texting?"

SKILLS
Microsoft Word, Excel, PowerPoint; plus FileMaker, Quark, Photoshop, Acrobat, WordPress

Note: All work projects cited in this resume were college-course assignments. Writing samples are available on request.

USE ACTION WORDS

Certain words evoke confidence and authority. When offering examples of past job requirements, be sure to start each sentence with an action word, like:

Achieved...
Assembled...
Assisted...
Built...
Cleaned...
Completed...
Convinced...
Created...
Delivered...
Designed...
Developed...
Equipped...
Established...
Experienced...
Guided...
Handled...
Learned...
Led...
Maintained...
Managed...
Operated...
Organized...
Performed...
Planned...
Produced...
Programmed...
Reduced...
Repaired...
Served...
Set up...
Sold...
Supervised...
Taught...
Trained...
Wrote...

Here's a sample resume showing work experience

Chris O. Hiremenow

3 Gimmeachance Road, Ourtown, US 00000

111/222-3333

GOAL

Seeking a position as a finish carpenter

EDUCATION

Certificate in Fine Carpentry, 06/2016

Tiger Maple Institute, Ourtown, US 00000

- Classes in architectural styles, technical drawing, furniture making, cabinet making

Diploma, 06/2014

Oakhurst Vocational School, Ourtown, US 00000

- Classes in construction techniques, hand tools, shop tools

WORK EXPERIENCE

Finish Carpenter, 06/2016 to Present

Hugh's High-End Homes, Ourtown, US 00000

- Duplicated existing English-style, oak-paneled walls for 350 sq/ft library expansion
- Designed and built 6'x9' replica Greek Revival fireplace mantle with hand-carved appliques
- Restored lower half of an Art-Deco staircase damaged by floodwaters
- Remodeled 20'x15' kitchen in the Nantucket style with deep coffered ceilings, bead-board cabinets, and wide pine floors
- Restored 12' high, salvaged antique Victorian doorway to original specifications

Assistant Finish Carpenter, 06/2014 to 06/2016

Arlene's Average Abodes, Ourtown, US 00000

- Installed windows, doors, trim, kitchen box cabinets, stairways, mantles on 15 homes

Intern, 01/2014 to 06/2014

Slap'em Up Houses, Ourtown, US 00000

- Helped install windows, doors, trim, and hardwood floors on 3 new homes

SKILLS

Replication, restoration, replacement, modification, design-build, CAD, hand tools, power tools, shop tools including laser cutters, shapers, planers

ADDITIONAL

Detail oriented, organized, neat, good sense of humor

You Try It

Your full name

Your address, city, state, zip code

Your phone, cell/text, email

GOAL

Give the job you are seeking

_____

EDUCATION

Give your diploma or degree and the date of award

_____

Give the school's name and city/state address

_____

· List several courses you took

_____

Repeat for additional schools or training

WORK HISTORY

Give your job title with beginning and ending dates

_____

Give your employer's name and city/state address

_____

· Give a job requirement, with an example

_____

· Give another job requirement, with an example

_____

· Give another job requirement, with an example

_____

· Give another job requirement, with an example

_____

· Give another job requirement, with an example

_____

Repeat for additional employers

SKILLS

Name the important tools, devices, procedures, programs, systems, and licenses you can operate or perform

_____

ADDITIONAL

Mention any special talents, abilities, or awards

_____

BASIC RESUME WRITING TIPS

- Use standard 8.5" by 11" white paper
- Keep a one-inch margin on all four sides of the page
- Avoid fancy fonts like outline, script, or other difficult-to-read styles
- Keep sentences short and to the point
- **Bold** or CAPITALIZE important headlines so they stand out
- Single space within sections
- Double space between sections
- Use bullets (·) at the beginning of a list
- Whenever possible, use numbers to show the size, volume, time, money, effort, or result of the projects you worked on
- Proofread for spelling and factual errors

© COPYRIGHT, HARRY DAHLSTROM

How people get job interviews

The job interview is your chance to sit down, face-to-face, with a hiring manager and convince her that she should hire you instead of someone else. How do you get a job interview? Here are some tips.

Employee referrals

Make a list of all the people you know who work in the same field or occupation as you.

Reach out to them. Ask if they could help you get a job interview where they work.

This is called networking—people connecting through other people. You are more likely to be hired if you have an employee connection.

In fact, most employers prefer to hire the friends of their workers. Eighty-eight percent of hiring managers say it's their best source for recruiting above-average candidates. Friends are so valuable, some employers will pay a finder's fee to an employee who brings in a new hire.

As the friend of an employee, you'll also have a special advantage over an outsider. Your inside friend can tell you about the hiring manager—her interviewing style, her management style, the issues she is most concerned about, the type of person she wants for the job, questions she is likely to ask, and the best way for you to ask for the job.

And here's an added bonus: Unlike answering a help-wanted ad or a job posting, where dozens of people might compete for the job, it's not uncommon for friends to be hired with little or no competition at all.

How to get started:

Call a friend. "Hi, Betty. It's Duncan."

Ask for some help. "I'd like to apply for a job as a baker at Bundt. I know that you work Bundt. On the job application, it asks if I know someone who works there. Would you mind if I mentioned, that you and I are friends?"

Three sources account for 76% of all new job hires
- Employee referrals create 39.9%
- Employer career sites create 21.2%
- Job boards create 14.6%

—Jobvite Index

Ask for information about the hiring manager. "Who is the bakery manager at Bundt? Is she the person I should send my resume to? What's she like?"

Ask for a special favor. "Could I ask a favor? Would you mind giving my resume to Ms. Pillsbury and putting in a good word for me?"

Show your gratitude. "Betty, thank you so much. If I get a job interview, I'll bake you a dozen dinner rolls."

Reach out to your old friends too

Research show that distant friends—former classmates, teammates, coworkers, and supervisors that you haven't seen in quite some time—but who work in the same field or industry as you, can be more useful than even your current friends.

These old friends have developed new friends, new connections, new information, and new insights that they could share with you.

They also know you and they trust you. They'd love to hear from you and catch up on the news. Reconnect with them. They live in a whole new world and they could open some new doors for you.

Employer career site

Do you have a list of favorite employers? Visit their web sites and see what kind of job openings they have.

How to get started:

Start with your favorite employer. Visit their web site and navigate to their employment page or career page.

Look through the job postings. Apply only for the jobs you are qualified to do. When you find a job that interests you, bookmark that web page so you can find your way back to it later.

Next, contact your friends. Ask if they know any mutual friends who work inside that company. Dig. You are 50 times more likely to get a job if you know an insider.

When you find an inside friend, ask if you could list him as a friend on your job application.

Then, ask a favor. Ask if he would give a copy of your resume to the hiring manager and put in a good word for you.

Be sure to thank your friend for his help and friendship.

Then, move on to the next employer on your favorite's list and repeat the process.

Job boards

Job boards like CareerBuilder, Monster, and CraigsList, plus job-search engines like Indeed and SimplyHired are very popular ways to find job openings.

But don't stop there. Check your area's online newspapers for help-wanted ads, plus the help ads posted on Twitter, Facebook, and LinkedIn too.

How to get started:

Submit a clean job application. Don't let misspellings, wrong numbers, missing information, and information typed in the wrong spaces disqualify you. See "job application," on page 32.

To boost your chances of getting a job interview, attach your resume and a cover letter with your job application. Your resume and cover letter offer a lot of information not asked in the job application. Writing a cover letter is fast and easy with AIDA—see the details on page 24.

CREATE A SIMPLE JOB-HUNTING PLAN

Every employer is not hiring today. You have to knock on a lot of doors to find the ones that are.

Here's a simple plan that takes only an hour or two a day. Give it a try and see how many interviews you can get.

- Monday through Friday, contact five employers every day. That's 25 employers a week, 100 a month. To reach them, use a good mix of all the ideas in this chapter.

- Now, you may not get a job interview the first week or so because it takes time for employers to respond.

- But, after two weeks, your phone should start to ring.

- When you begin to get job interviews, don't stop contacting five new employers every day. Stick with your plan right up until the day you accept a job offer.

- If you do stop, your flow of interviews will dry up in about two weeks. Then it will take you two more weeks to get the pipeline flowing again.

© COPYRIGHT, HARRY DAHLSTROM

Walk-ins

One of the easiest ways to get a job interview is to look for "Now Hiring" signs on business buildings, doorways, and billboards.

How to get started:

Walk into the shop, store, or office. Smile, and ask one of the employees if you can fill out a job application. You might say, "Hi, I saw your now-hiring sign. May I have a job application, please?"

Then, ask a few questions to show your interest. You might simply ask, "Which jobs are available? What are the duties of a yodeler? Which days and hours are available?"

Try to get an inside referral. The best way to get a job is to get someone who works inside the company to put in a good word for you. So, while you're in the office, ask the employee if someone from your neighborhood, school, or former employer works there.

If you know the insider, call him when you get home. Mention that you applied for a job where he works. Ask if he could give your resume to the hiring manager and put in a good word for you.

If you don't know any insiders, contact your friends and relatives. See if they know an insider who might be able to help.

Job fairs and open-houses

Where can you meet dozens of recruiters, face to face, all in one day, all in one place? Simple. Go to a job fair or a company open house. Recruiters are standing there, waiting to meet you.

Keep in mind that recruiters do not usually hire people at career fairs. The fair or open-house is an opportunity for them to meet job hunters,

collect resumes, and schedule job interviews. They prefer not to interview at the job fair because the fairs are noisy, fast paced, and there are too many people to interview. So they usually schedule interviews which take place a few days after the fair.

To find an event in your area, Google Job Fair, Career Fair, and Company Open House. Also, check for open-house announcements in the help-wanted section of your Sunday newspapers. Oh, and check with your school's career center and your local American Job Center to see if they're planning a job fair (see page 23).

How to get started:

- Once you are inside the job fair, walk up to the employer's table or booth.

- Make eye contact with the recruiter, smile, and say hello. Offer your handshake and introduce yourself.

- Deliver your "sales pitch" from page 23.

- Answer the recruiter's questions.

- Offer the recruiter a copy of your resume.

- Ask for the recruiter's business card.

- Ask how you can schedule a job interview.

- Thank the recruiter for speaking with you, smile, and offer your handshake.

When you get home, reintroduce yourself by sending the recruiter a thank-you note and another copy of your resume. Use the cover letter template starting on page 24. All of the recruiter's contact information is on her business card. The thank-you note tells the recruiter that you do want an interview and you took the time to follow-up and ask for one.

Temporary employment agencies

Temporary employment agencies are match

makers. They bring together employers that need help and job hunters who need work.

Working for a temp agency is a great way to get your foot in the door at a good company. You'll learn new skills, gain experience, make contacts, and build references. Every year, about 9 million people find work through employment agencies—and 79 percent are placed in full-time positions.

How to get started:

Google "Employment Agencies" for a list of agencies in your area. You might also ask your friends if they've ever worked with an employment agency. Maybe a friend can recommend a good agency for you.

Call an agency and ask to register for employment. The agent will ask a few questions about your background and skills. If you are a good fit for the agency, the agent will ask you to come in for a meeting.

During the meeting, the agent will go over your resume and ask questions about your skills and abilities. For some occupations, like secretarial or graphic design, the agent may ask you to take a skills test to measure your abilities.

The agent will also ask about your needs. Do you want to work for a large company or a small one? How far are you willing to commute? Do you want full-time, part-time, or seasonal work? What wage or salary do you expect?

The agent will then try to match you to a job opening at one of their employer clients.

Job Centers and Career Centers

The six activities we just discussed are do-it-yourself activities. You can use those activities to contact an employer yourself.

But, what if you'd like some help? What if you'd like to talk to someone about career counsel-

ing, how the job market works, who the major employers are, have someone look over your resume or job application, tell you about upcoming job fairs, or offer some interviewing tips?

Well, there are employment counselors you can talk with. Here are two great resources that have helped millions of people find work—

· **American Job Centers.** Your state government operates a number of Job Centers. They are open to the public *and their services are free.*

· **School Career Centers.** Most schools and colleges have career centers. Their services are available to their students and alumni, and their services are also free.

Lots of employers are loyal to local Job Centers and Career Centers and they regularly post job openings and recruit new hires there. Job counselors have good working relationships with recruiters, hiring managers, and business owners. This relationship between job counselors and local employers can help open doors to job interviews for you.

How to get started:

Call or visit your local Job Center and Career Center. Ask to speak with an employment counselor. Explain what kind of work you're looking for. Ask if the counselor could give you a few referrals—the names of recruiters, hiring managers, or business owners who are hiring people with your skills.

Once you have their names, send a letter or an email, plus your resume, to introduce yourself to each person. Use the cover letter format starting on page 24. A few days later, follow-up with a phone call to see if they received your letter—and ask for a job interview.

To find your state's local job center, Google— *American Job Centers,* or *One Stop Career Centers.*

CREATE A 15 SECOND SALES PITCH

A sales pitch is a short speech. It's a 15 second "sound bite" that sells you to hiring managers and anyone who can help you get a job interview.

A good sales pitch includes your name, your occupation, your accomplishments, your goal, and your UPS (Unique Selling Point). Your UPS is what separates you from the competition.

Spend some time thinking about your sales pitch. Here's a good example to go by:

"Hi, my name is Mason Stone."

"I've been an apprentice stone mason for the past year and I've learned both wet and dry masonry."

"I've built walkways, terraces, retaining walls, and patios for residential customers. They've been very happy with my work."

"Now, I'm looking for a full-time junior masonry job."

"Let me also add that—I'm a hard worker and I give more than a minimum effort. I'm reliable and I'll show up on time every day. I'm a quick learner and I'm easy to coach. I also have a good sense of humor and I get along with people. I would love to interview with your company."

© COPYRIGHT, HARRY DAHLSTROM

How to write a better cover letter

A cover letter is a personal letter that you send with your resume or job application. It's the first thing the hiring manager sees when she opens your envelope or email. It's your hello, your smile, your chance to create a rapport, your reason for writing.

Q. "Does everyone send a cover letter with their resume or job application?"

No. Most people don't include a cover letter. And that's why you should send one. It shows that you're different. It shows that you are serious about the job and you cared enough to write.

Q. "Do I have to create a new letter each time I apply to a different company?"

Yes and no. You certainly want all employers to feel that you are writing to them personally. But, you can recycle paragraphs and include them in most of your letters.

Q. "Who should I address my letter to?"

This is important—the hiring manager is usually the manager of the department where you want to work. If you want a job in human resources, send your letter to the human-resource manager. If you want to work in maintenance, send you letter to the maintenance manager. At a small business, send your letter to the owner of the business.

Q. "How do I get the manager's name?"

If you are getting a referral from a friend, ask your friend for the hiring manager's name. When writing, address your letter and envelope to that manager by name and title: Ms. Iva Joboffer, IT Manager. Make sure the manager's name, title, and address are accurate and spelled correctly.

If you are writing to a company and you don't know the manager's name, call the company. The receptionist who answers your call will be glad to give you the information you need.

If you are answering an advertisement or job posting that gives no contact person's name or no company name, address your letter to *Hiring Manager.*

Eighty-six percent of executives said cover letters are important when evaluating job candidates.

—National Association of Workforce Development Professionals

Q. "How long does my cover letter have to be?"

Keep your cover letter short and simple. One page is perfect.

Q. "Could you help me write my letter?"

You bet. But first, I'd like you to meet AIDA.

Q. "Who's AIDA?"

The folks who write professional sales letters use a magic formula. It's called AIDA. That's short for—Attention, Interest, Desire, Action.

AIDA sells billions of dollars worth of goods and services every year. If it can work for business, it can work for you. So, let's use AIDA to convince a hiring manager to give you a job interview.

1. Attention

In the very first paragraph of your letter, grab the hiring manager's attention simply by telling her why you are writing. Below are several solid reasons for writing to a hiring manager. Adapt the ONE that works best for you.

· "I would like to apply for the sous chef's position I saw advertised in..."

· "My friend, Frieda Friendly, works in your department. She recommended that I write to you."

· "I stumbled upon your website. Wow. I'd like to interview for a position with your firm because..."

· "I shop at your store and..."

· "We met at a job fair on..."

· "I would like to learn about the career opportunities for mechanics at your shop."

2. Interest

In the second paragraph of your letter, rouse the manager's interest by explaining what makes you special. Here are a few examples. Adapt the ONE that works best for you.

· "I have three-years experience as a..."

· "I worked on the Slingshot project at David's and..."

· "I just graduated from school and..."

· "I have three special abilities I can bring to the job..."

· "I have an idea I'd like to discuss with you..."

3. Desire

If you are responding to a help-wanted advertisement or a job posting, be sure to talk about the job requirements the ad says are important. Otherwise, create a desire for the hiring manager to meet you by offering three solid accomplishments.

· "I am very familiar with..."

· "I know how to use..."

· "I also have experience with..."

4. Action

Finally, ask the hiring manager for a job interview. Adapt ONE of the following statements that works best for you.

· "I would like to interview for your nursing position. Please call. You can reach me anytime on my cell at 555-666-7777."

· "I would like to interview for your nursing position. I hope you won't mind if I call in a few days to see that you received my resume and hopefully to schedule an interview."

NOT GETTING A GOOD RESPONSE FROM ALL THE HELP-WANTED ADS AND NETWORKING YOU'VE TRIED?

Maybe you should try some old-school job hunting.

Suppose you want to work for SawBuck Bank. Mail the hiring manager a letter through the US Postal Service and ask for a job interview.

Or, suppose you want to work for any bank. Why not pull together a list of all the banks in your area and mail each manager a letter asking for a job interview?

You could do this with the employers in your industry too.

Start by assembling a list of 25 employers that you would like to contact this week. Include plenty of small, medium, and large employers. The idea is to target 5 employers each day, Monday through Friday. That's 25 employers a week—100 a month.

Send each manager a copy of your resume and a short cover-letter explaining what makes you different from all the other job hunters out there.

You never know which employers are thinking of hiring someone new. So, send them all a letter and a resume. You could get a job interview before the job opening goes public.

A sample letter using AIDA

Your name and contact information ▶

Pat Perfect
One Pluperfect Way
Anytown, US 12345
(111) 222-3333
pat@email.com

Date ▶

December 31, 20xx

Hiring manager's name and address ▶

Ms. Karin K. Boom, Owner
New Day Demolitions, Inc.
55 Nowhiring Highway
Anytown, US 12345

Job Code ▶

Re: Job Code 5678, from the *Blabbermouth*

Salutation ▶

Dear Ms. Boom:

Attention ▶

I would like to apply for your Office Receptionist's position, which I saw advertised in Wednesday's edition of the *Blabbermouth.*

Interest ▶

Ms. Boom, I can offer you three years of experience as a receptionist. I have a cheerful helpful personality, and I have a good memory for names, faces, voices, and telephone numbers.

Desire ▶

· I am familiar with most telephone systems, social media, email, plus both Apple and Microsoft operating systems.

· I have hands-on experience with QuickBooks, Microsoft Word, Excel, and appointment scheduling software.

· I also have experience as a bill collector. If the need arises, I would be happy to make collection calls or field difficult or awkward inquiries.

Action ▶

I would love to interview for this position. I hope you'll call. You can reach me anytime on my cell at (111) 222-3333.

When you do call, please understand that the child's voice on my voice-mail greeting is not my voice!

I look forward to your call.

Closing ▶

Sincerely,

Signature ▶

Pat Perfect

Printed name ▶

Pat Perfect

You Try It

Your name
Your address
Your city, state, zip
Your phone number
Your email address

Today's date

Manager's name and title
Department's name
Company's name
Address
City, state, zip

Re: (Job code, if listed in an ad or job posting)

Dear (Mr. or Ms.):

Get the manager's attention

_____

_____

Rouse the manager's interest

_____

_____

Create a desire to meet you

. _____

. _____

. _____

Ask the manager to take action

_____

_____

Sincerely,

Your Signature

Pat Perfect

Prepare for the hiring manager's phone call

You've found a job opening and applied for the position. Now, if the hiring manager likes what she sees in your resume, she'll give you a call. Don't underestimate the importance of this phone call. It's actually a screening interview. The purpose of the call is to decide whether to invite you to a face-to-face job interview. Here are five tips to help you pass the screen and win an invitation to the interview.

1. Have a professional greeting

You never know when an employer might call, so answer every phone call with a professional greeting. Sure, your friends will laugh when they call and hear you say, "Hello. This is Ken Dooit. How can I help you?" But the hiring managers will love it.

Also, record a new phone message. Something short and professional like this—"Hello. This is Ken Dooit. I'm not able to answer the phone. Please leave your name, phone number, and a brief message. I do check my messages often. I'll return your call as soon as possible. Thank you."

2. When they call, most hiring managers will ask if this is a convenient time to speak with you.

Managers know that you have a life. If you're at work, driving your car, or sitting in the dentist's chair, it's okay to arrange another time to talk.

When you return a call, choose a place where you'll be free from noise, interruptions, and where your cell phone has good reception.

You might say—

"Good afternoon, Ms. Hireyou. My name is Ken Dooit. I'm returning your phone call. I applied for a job as a tight-rope walker."

3. Don't wing it

Prepare and rehearse like this is a real interview. Because it is. If you bomb this screening interview, you won't get the face-to-face interview or the job offer.

So, be prepared. Have your resume, cover letter, job advertisement, and notes from the employer's website in front of you.

10

Your telephone conversation with a hiring manager could last between ten minutes and an hour.

—*Wall Street Journal*

You can't know which questions a hiring manager might ask, so look over these common questions plus those on page 44.

· Are you currently employed? Where?

· What is your job title?

· How long have you been working there?

· What are your duties and responsibilities?

· Tell me about your job skills.

· Do you get along with your supervisor?

· Why are you leaving?

· When are you available to begin work?

· Why do you want to work for my company?

· What motivates you to do a good job?

· What are your career goals?

4. Relax

Try to visualize what the manager looks like based on the sound of his or her voice—maybe a favorite cousin, a friend, or teacher. This will help make the manager seem more familiar and less intimidating.

Don't forget to smile—even on the phone. Smiling helps project a personality that comes across in your voice. You should also stand up while speaking on the phone and use your hands to gesture. Thinking on your feet and gesturing helps with your thought processes. They'll also help slow down your speech so you don't slur your words and start to spit.

5. Watch your manners

Always refer to the manager as Mr. or Ms., unless the hiring manager asks you to use their first name. Be sure to say please and thank you.

Don't sip a drink, chew gum, or nibble on food, the manager will hear it and it's rude.

Don't use foul or inappropriate language—this is the workplace not the schoolyard.

Try not to say, "No problem," "Uh-huh," "Like," or "Ya know," too often. They can become annoying.

Also, don't ask about money, benefits, or vacations—they are usually discussed when a job offer is made.

Be willing to accept the hiring manager's interview schedule, even if you have to reschedule the cable guy.

Confirm the date and time of the interview by repeating it back to the hiring manager—"That's Thursday the 13th at 3:13..."

Thank the hiring manager for showing an interest in you—"Ms. Hireyou, thank you so much for this opportunity. I look forward to meeting you on Thursday. Bye."

And here's a big one. Don't take another phone call or try to read your text messages during this phone interview. It's the #1 reason a hiring manager will hang up on you. So, turn off the dings and rings before your phone interview begins. Let the manager feel that she is your most important phone call.

Okay, one more tip

If the manager doesn't offer you a job interview, ask for one. That's what this phone call is all about. You might say something as simple as this—"I'm very interested in this position. I would love to visit your company. Could we schedule an interview?"

DON'T LET YOUR SOCIAL-MEDIA SITES KEEP AN EMPLOYER FROM CALLING YOU

A CareerBuilder/Harris Poll reports that most hiring managers will Google a job applicant's name to see if he or she has a social media presence on Facebook, LinkedIn, Twitter, and other sites.

Hiring managers aren't looking for negative information. They simply want to get a sense of the job applicant's personality.

A friendly and helpful online personality, a professional image, good communication skills, and a little creativity will make a very nice impression.

However, inappropriate photographs, content about drug and alcohol use, bad-mouthing a previous employer or coworker, vile language, and negative comments about race, religion, or gender are real turn-offs.

Some hiring managers will even ask to friend or follow the job applicant. This can open the door to the job applicant's private pages. So, be careful what you allow people to see on your social media pages—it can affect whether a hiring manager chooses to call you or not.

© COPYRIGHT, HARRY DAHLSTROM

Find three people who will give you a positive recommendation

You are a good worker. You give more than the minimum. You show up everyday and you're never late. You're easy going and everybody likes you. Well, that's great, but the hiring manager wants proof. She wants to talk to three references, three people who can vouch for you.

Q. "Who should I include as references?"

Most hiring managers want three reliable references. Ideally, they want the name of your current boss—but NOT if that boss doesn't know that you're looking for another job. In that case, they'll want the name of your previous employer.

Other good references might include former supervisors, coworkers, customers, teachers, coaches, and prominent people who know you. Prominent people might include an attorney, a banker, a doctor, a member of the clergy, or a local business owner.

Q. "Am I supposed to ask before offering someone's name as a job reference?"

Yes. Always ask. People who agree to serve as references almost always give a better recommendation than those who are not asked.

Those who are NOT asked are often caught off guard. They might struggle to remember who you are, what you did, and when you worked for them. To a hiring manager this hesitation might sound like your reference is not eager to recommend you.

Q. "How do I ask someone to be a reference? What do I say?"

Call or visit them. Don't ask by text or email. You need to see each person's face or hear their voice when you ask.

Eighty percent of employers said they regularly conduct reference checks.

—The Society for Human Resource Management

When you do ask, don't just ask for a recommendation. Ask for a "positive recommendation."

You might say, "Elmer, I'm applying for work as a ballerina. I would like to list you as a reference. Would you be able to give me a positive recommendation?"

Most people are flattered when asked. They'll be happy to give you a good recommendation and they'll say so.

Others might not be interested in singing your praises. So, listen to their voice. Notice their body language. What does your gut tell you? If you don't think they'll give you a good recommendation, don't use them.

Q. "I know my former boss won't give me a good recommendation. Do I have to list him as a reference?"

Could you ask your boss's boss for a recommendation instead?

Q. "Maybe I should just tell the hiring manager that my boss and I didn't get along."

The manager will admire your honesty.

Here's a big tip—never badmouth a former boss. It screams that you are a troublemaker.

Instead, put a positive spin on a negative situation. Try this: "Mr. Pumpernickel was the most demanding boss I ever worked for. We had our moments. But, I learned more from him than anyone I've ever worked for. I'll probably miss him."

Q. "Should I list my references on my resume?"

No. Your resume will pass through lots of hands— friends, friends-of-friends, and probably a few people you might not even know. You don't want the names of your references to fall into the wrong hands. So, keep them off your resume. Another thing, if you put your references on your resume, you are inviting hiring managers to call your references before they've even met you.

Instead, list your references on a separate sheet of paper. Include each person's name, address, phone number, employer, job title, and best times for the hiring manager to call. Hand your list of references to the hiring manager during your job interview.

Q. "Should I send my references a copy of my resume?"

Yes. Don't let them struggle to remember who you are and what you did on the job.

Once someone agrees to give you a positive reference, refresh his or her memory of you. Send a copy of your resume plus a list of the projects or assignments you worked on together. Be sure to include your duties, responsibilities, accomplishments and any other information that might help them write a good recommendation for you.

QUESTIONS A HIRING MANAGER MIGHT ASK YOUR REFERENCES

- Were you Heidi Hopeful's immediate supervisor?
- What was Heidi's job title?
- What were her dates of employment?
- What were her duties and responsibilities?
- What were her most significant accomplishments?
- Did Heidi receive any promotions or awards?
- What was Heidi's attitude toward work?
- What was her level of energy at work?
- Did she get along with her coworkers and managers?
- How often was she late or absent?
- What were her job strengths?
- In which skills does Heidi need improvement?
- Why did Heidi leave the job?
- If possible, would you rehire her?
- Is there anything I didn't ask you, that I should have asked?

© COPYRIGHT, HARRY DAHLSTROM

How to fill out a job application

On the next few pages, you'll find questions commonly asked on most job applications. Use these pages to create a "copy sheet" with accurate dates, names, addresses, and numbers. Later, when you fill out a real job application you won't struggle to remember the facts. You can simply copy the information from these pages.

If you haven't completed the company's standard job application yet, you'll be asked to fill out one before your job interview begins.

The application is part of the paperwork. It's a record that shows you applied for a job. It's also a legal document— you are asked to sign a statement giving the employer permission to check the facts in your application.

Even if you have a resume, be a good sport and complete the full application. Don't sluff off your answers by writing, "Please see the attached resume." It can be seen as arrogant.

The way you complete the application makes a statement about the kind of worker you are.

A complete, accurate, and neat application says that you take pride in your work.

Missing information and information entered in the wrong spaces, says that you didn't follow the instructions.

Misspelled names, partial addresses, wrong telephone numbers, and missing dates, say that you came unprepared.

Exaggerations make a statement about your truthfulness. When sitting across from the hiring manager, you don't want to be put in the awkward spot of having to admit that you embellished on some of your answers.

Read the application carefully before you start. If you don't understand a question, ask for help. If a question does not apply to you, write "Not Applicable," or "N.A." in the space.

Sixty-five percent of employers say that the best way to apply for an open position is through the employment page of their company's web site.

—The Society for Human Resource Management

A PRACTICE APPLICATION FOR EMPLOYMENT
PART 1. APPLICANT INFORMATION

Last name	First name		Middle initial
Address	City	State	Zip
Telephone	Email or text address		
Social Security Number			

Are you 18 years of age or older?	☐ Yes	☐ No	
Are you a citizen of the United States?	☐ Yes	☐ No	
Are you legally eligible for employment in the United States?	☐ Yes	☐ No	

Have you served in the Armed Forces of the United States?   ☐ Yes   ☐ No

If "Yes" give dates	Branch of service	Highest rank
Duties		

Are you now a member of the National Guard or the Reserves?   ☐ Yes   ☐ No

If "Yes" give dates	Branch of service	Rank
Duties		

PART 2. EMPLOYMENT DESIRED

What position are you seeking?   Wage or salary expected

Note: Do not give a wage or salary. You might look unreasonable if it's too large, or look desperate if it's too low. Instead, write "Standard wage."

Are you seeking: ☐ Full-time work   ☐ Part-time work   ☐ Seasonal work

When can you begin work?

Can you work weekends?	☐ Yes	☐ No
Can you work evenings?	☐ Yes	☐ No
Are you available for overtime?	☐ Yes	☐ No
If hired, will you have reliable transportation to and from work?	☐ Yes	☐ No

How were you referred to us?

☐ Friend or relative   ☐ "Now hiring" sign
☐ Our website   ☐ Newspaper advertisement
☐ American Job Center   ☐ Radio or TV advertisement
☐ School placement office   ☐ Job fair
☐ Careerbuilder, Indeed, etc.   ☐ Employment agency
     ☐ Other

Have you been employed with us in the past?   ☐ Yes   ☐ No

If "Yes," please give the following

Your job title	Supervisor's name
Department	Work address
Dates of employment	Reason for leaving

© COPYRIGHT, HARRY DAHLSTROM

INFORMATION YOU'LL NEED TO COMPLETE A JOB APPLICATION

Your Information
· Your legal name
· Address
· Telephone
· Email
· Social Security Number
· Work permits
· Work licenses

Employee Friend
· Friend's name
· Job title
· Department
· Address
· Telephone

Each School
· School's name
· Address
· Telephone
· Your date of completion or attendance
· Degree, award, or major

Former Employers
· Company's name
· Address
· Telephone
· Your job title
· Begin/End dates
· Duties
· Supervisor's name

Three References
· Names
· Job titles
· Addresses
· Phone numbers
· Best times to call

Do you have a friend or relative employed by us? ☐ Yes ☐ No

Note: If you do, call your friend and ask if you can put his or her name on your job application. Also ask if she would put in a good word for you. Having an inside referral is one of the best ways to get a job.

If "Yes," please provide the following information about your friend:

Person's name	Job title
Department	Work address
Phone	

PART 3. EDUCATION

High school attended

School's name			
Address	City	State	Zip
Years completed	Did you receive a diploma/GED? ☐ Yes ☐ No		
Program or specialty	Grade Point Average (GPA):		
Sports/Clubs/Groups			

College, university, or other post-secondary school attended

School's name			
Address	City	State	Zip
Years completed	Degree or certification awarded		
Program or specialty	Grade Point Average (GPA)		
Sports/Clubs/Groups			

PART 4. EMPLOYMENT

Note: If you have no formal work experience, don't panic. Instead, list the informal jobs you've had—volunteer, charitable, self-employment, freelance or homemaker. You can even list casual jobs like coaching, tutoring, baby-sitting, or mowing lawns ·

Current or last employer

Company name			
Address	City	State	Zip
Your job title	Your hourly wage or salary		
Begin date	End date		

Note: When listing your duties, include numbers from your resume on page 12 to turn your duties into accomplishments.

Your duties

Supervisor's name	May we contact him or her? ☐ Yes ☐ No
Supervisor's telephone number	
Your reason for leaving	

Previous employer

Company name			
Address	City	State	Zip
Your job title	Your hourly wage or salary		
Begin date	End date		
Your duties			

Supervisor's name	May we contact him or her? ☐ Yes ☐ No
Supervisor's telephone number	
Your reason for leaving	

Previous employer

Company name

Address	City	State	Zip

Your job title	Your hourly wage or salary

Begin date	End date

Your duties

Supervisor's name	May we contact him or her? ☐ Yes ☐ No

Supervisor's telephone number

Your reason for leaving

PART 5. REFERENCES

Note: A reference is someone who can testify to your character and abilities. Managers, supervisors, coworkers, customers, teachers, coaches, clergy, public officials, business leaders, and others are acceptable references. Again, before you offer anyone's name as a reference, make sure you have that person's permission.

Personal reference #1

Person's name	Telephone

Address	City	State	Zip

How do you know this person?	Best time to call?

Personal reference #2

Person's name	Telephone

Address	City	State	Zip

How do you know this person?	Best time to call?

Personal reference #3

Person's name	Telephone

Address	City	State	Zip

How do you know this person?	Best time to call?

PART 6. ADDITIONAL INFORMATION

Please list any special skills, languages, qualifications, accomplishments, certifications, or licenses you have that were not previously mentioned

Please give any additional information you feel may be helpful when considering your application

PART 7. PLEASE READ CAREFULLY BEFORE SIGNING

I understand that this application for employment will be given every consideration, but its receipt does not constitute a contract of employment, nor does it imply that I will be hired.

I certify that all answers given on this employment application are true and complete. I also understand and agree that any false information may be grounds for termination of my employment at any point in the future if I am hired.

I understand that all information on this job application is subject to verification. I authorize and give my consent for Ajax Company to contact my references, educational institutions, previous employers, and to conduct all other necessary background checks.

I hereby acknowledge that I have read and understand this agreement.

Signature	Printed name	Date

BACKGROUND CHECKS

Most employers will try to verify the information given in your job application, resume, and job interview. Unless your state has legal restrictions, employers may also request or obtain the following information:

- Address history
- Character references
- Court records
- Credit records
- Driving records
- Drug tests
- Education records
- Employment history
- Licensing records
- Military records
- Neighbor interviews
- Past employers
- Personal references
- Sex offender lists
- Social Security Number
- Work permits
- Workers' compensation claims

© COPYRIGHT, HARRY DAHLSTROM

What to wear to a job interview

Think about this—when you meet someone new, you size him or her up. In about a minute, you can decide whether or not you like the person. Well, hiring managers are good at sizing people up too. They see lots of job applicants and they can tell in a flash who will fit in and who will not. In a job interview, the goal is to show that you fit in—and the first thing a hiring manager will notice is how you look. Here's how to make a good, first impression:

Start with a good night's sleep

Employers expect to meet someone who is enthusiastic, energetic, and excited to be there.

Shower

It will help you look sharp, alert, and healthy.

Shampoo your hair

One of the first things the manager will look at is your hair. It makes a huge statement about your overall hygiene and cleanliness.

Brush your teeth

Get the manager to remember your ideas, your skills, your personality—not what you had for breakfast. Brush, floss, and use a mouthwash.

Use deodorant and an antiperspirant

The manager will think that you're as cool as a cucumber. Rub a little on your hands and you'll have a smooth dry handshake too.

Use eye drops

Get the red out and let your eyes twinkle.

Trim your nails

Guys, long fingernails are a turn off. Most hiring managers will notice when they reach to shake your hand. Ladies, hiring managers won't be impressed if long nails prevent you from doing the work.

Hair styles

Choose a simple style that makes you look good. Get the manager to focus on your face, your expressions, your eyes—not your hair style.

Right or wrong, people do make assumptions based on the way we dress. In 3 to 5 seconds, they make judgements about our confidence, character, income and sociability.

—Psychology Today

Avoid strong perfumes or colognes

Some people may find it unpleasant.

Makeup

In business, less is more. The idea is to look professional so you'll be taken seriously.

Shave

Guys, a two-day stubble looks great on the weekend, but not in a job interview. Showing up with stubble means you didn't shave.

Body piercings

One or two piercings are fine. A half dozen or more becomes a distraction. Tongue jewelry can also be a distraction.

Avoid trendy fashions

It's been said that fashion gets attention—but it doesn't convey power. Classic clothing conveys power. Conduct your job interview from a point of strength, not novelty.

Dress in the clothes that you would wear on the job

Executives should wear business suits. Office people should wear dress clothes. Workers should wear work clothes. If you're not sure what to wear to your interview, call the company and ask someone in their human resources office. They'll be glad to tell you.

You can't go wrong with the classic white-collar outfits

For men—navy-blue blazer, gray slacks, white shirt, striped tie, black lace-up shoes, black socks, and a black dress belt. For women—a charcoal gray or navy skirt or pantsuit, white blouse, scarf or necklace, with black pumps, black hose, black belt, and a simple black bag.

Check your clothes

Make sure they fit properly and feel comfortable. Check for holes, tears, splits, stains, missing buttons, runs, frayed hems, worn cuffs, puckers, pulls, or wrinkles.

Wear clean, freshly pressed clothes

Send your jacket, skirt, and pants off to be dry-cleaned and pressed. Have your shirt or blouse laundered, starched, and pressed. Looking sharp tells the manager that you take pride in your appearance and your work.

Avoid excessive jewelry

For men, a wristwatch and a ring are plenty. For women, a watch, a ring, a necklace, and a pair of earrings are ideal.

Avoid bright colors, loud fashions, and patterns that clash

Again, it's a sign that you need lots of attention.

Empty your pockets

No bulges to ruin your profile and no jingling change to fall out of your pocket when you sit down for your interview.

Smile—smile big

You're beautiful. Take a picture!

BEFORE YOU HEAD OUT THE DOOR...

Never bring anyone with you to a job interview. Go alone. If someone gives you a ride, ask him or her to wait in the car.

Bring several copies of your resume and carry them in a simple manila folder.

Bring a typed list with three personal references, including their names, addresses, telephone numbers, how you know them, and best times to call.

Bring two forms of identification.

Bring your Social Security Number.

Bring your work permits and visas.

Bring work samples or your portfolio if needed.

Bring money for gas, tolls, parking or public transportation.

Bring a new note pad and a pen that works.

Write the manager's name, department, address, and telephone number in the note pad—just in case.

Plan to arrive 10 minutes before the interview begins. When you arrive check in with the receptionist. Visit the rest room to check your appearance.

If something happens and you are going to be late, call the manager and explain what happened.

© COPYRIGHT, HARRY DAHLSTROM

Enthusiasm, the key to a great interview

Hiring managers agree—enthusiasm separates the winners from the losers. It can be more important than experience. "Give me someone who's enthusiastic and motivated," explained one manager, "someone who's alert and alive... someone who's interested in what we do here... someone who's excited about coming to work for me... someone who wants to help me as much as I want to help them."

You don't need to become one of the loud, back-slapping types

Just be you.

Plan to arrive ten-minutes early for your interview

It shows that you are excited to be there. Hiring managers are clock-watchers. They'll notice.

Be extra courteous

Say hello, smile, and be friendly to everyone you meet. You can bet that the manager will ask what they thought of you, after you've left the building.

Offer a professional greeting

When you meet the manager, stand up straight, look her in the eye, smile, extend a firm handshake, and say, "Ms. Joboffer, thank you so much for taking the time to interview me for your cat-herding position."

About that handshake

Engage the full hand, palm to palm. Grip firmly to show that you mean it, but don't crush. Look the other person in the eye. Smile. Pump two or three times. Release.

Don't undersell yourself and don't oversell yourself. Sales people who are middle-verts outsell introverts by 29 percent and outsell extraverts by 24 percent.

—Adam Grant, University of Pennsylvania

Show respect for the manager's position

Address the manager as Mr. or Ms., unless they ask you to call them by their first name. Once you're in the manager's office, don't sit down until you're invited to sit. Be sure to look at the manager whenever she speaks.

Show some curiosity

Ask for a short tour of the workplace before the interview begins. Look around. Ask questions about the cool things you see. Talk shop—ask what the manager thinks of the latest software, the newest gadget, or the hot new trend in your industry.

Have a sense of humor

We are drawn to happy, optimistic, humorous people. When appropriate, offer a clever quip, a one-liner, or an interesting tale. Keep it short, positive and upbeat. Don't forget to chuckle at the manager's attempts at humor.

Think, "can do"

If a manager says you don't have a certain skill or enough experience, don't just shrug your shoulders. Most managers want to see whether you'll fight for what you want or whether you'll just give up.

So, tell the hiring manager that you're a quick learner, a hard worker, and that you always deliver more than what's expected. Let her know that you will become one of the best employees she will ever hire.

Let your body language do some talking

Sit up straight. Sit near the edge of the chair with both feet on the floor. Visualize your ideas and use your hands to illustrate what you

mean. Look the manager in the eye. Use facial expressions to emphasize important points.

Show a little empathy

Empathy means that you understand how the other person feels. When the manager talks about an important issue, look at her eyes to show that you are listening, use facial expressions to show that you understand, and ask for details to show that you care.

Have a reason for wanting to work there

Visit the company's website and Google the company name for news. Find out who they are, what they do, and why you want to work there.

Participate in the conversation

The interview should be a 50/50 conversation. Don't be a motor-mouth who never stops talking. And don't be a zombie who hardly says a word. Listen. Ask questions. Give generous answers.

Become a storyteller

You probably have a great reason for choosing your line of work. When the manager asks, "What made you decide to become a puppeteer?"—tell your story. Include lots of detail and use body language to bring your story to life.

TRY A LITTLE MIRRORING

Mirroring is a body-language dance where you copy the hiring manager's actions. It creates a bond. It says, "We're in sync."

Mirroring is not new. Everybody does it. If you smile at someone, they'll usually smile back. Like the smile, most mirroring is unintentional. But, if you are aware of mirroring, you can boost its effectiveness.

Here are some simple mirroring tips:

- When the hiring manager smiles or frowns, you should smile or frown too.
- If the manager uses hand gestures to add emphasis, you should use hand gestures when you want to add emphasis.
- If the manager sits up straight or leans toward you, you should sit straight or lean too.
- If the manager speaks quickly or slowly, you should match her pace when speaking.
- If the manager uses special job-related words or technical terms, you should use them too.

© COPYRIGHT, HARRY DAHLSTROM

Navigate your way through a job interview

Managers are expert interviewers and they know that you're going to be nervous. To help you relax and feel comfortable, they'll conduct the interview as if it were a casual, friendly conversation. Now, each manager has her own style and personality. There is no set format to a job interview. But there is a beginning, a middle, and an end. So, let's walk through the interview from beginning to end and see how it unfolds.

Your arrival

Come prepared for each interview. Don't wing it. Visit the company's website. Know who they are, what they do, and have a good reason why you want to work there.

When you first arrive, check in with the receptionist. Smile and introduce yourself. You might say, "Hi, my name is Luke Atmenow. I have a 4:14 appointment with Ms. Ida Hireyou in the imagineering department. When you have a moment could you please let her know that I'm here? Thank you."

If you're wearing a winter coat or a raincoat, ask where you can hang your coat. Don't bring it into the interview with you. You'll look awkward carrying it. Plus, carrying a coat gives the impression that this is a quick meeting and you'll be in and out in just a few minutes. Besides, what will you do with it once you're in the hiring manager's office? It's best if you hang your coat in the waiting room.

After checking your coat, visit the restroom. Check your hair, teeth, clothes and turn off your phone. Some hiring managers say they would not hire someone who took a cell call during a job interview.

Oh, while you're in the restroom, try this. Lock your self into a stall. Then, strike the Superman pose. You know, feet apart, standing tall, hands on your hips, gazing upward. Hold that pose for two full minutes. You could walk into the interview feeling like you could change the world.

Seriously. A Harvard psychologist found that

55

The average job interview lasts about 55 minutes. Interviews for management-level positions last about 86 minutes.

—Robert Half Recruitment

power posing reduced stress and increased confidence by about 20 percent.

Okay. Looking good? Feeling good? Phone turned off? Take a seat in waiting area. Sit up straight. Try not to fidget. Run through the interview in your mind. Visualize the important parts—like an athlete might visualize an upcoming event.

The greeting

The hiring manager will usually come into the waiting area to meet you. Sometimes an assistant will greet you and escort you to hiring manager's office.

Either way, when someone mentions your name, stand up. Smile and say, "Hi, I'm Luke Atmenow." The hiring manager will smile, walk toward you and introduce herself.

Offer your handshake and say, "It's so nice to meet you, Ms. Hireyou. Thank you for inviting me to this interview." Saying her name will help you remember it.

As you are escorted to the hiring manager's office, make small talk to show that you are friendly and sociable.

Big tip: Find something other than the weather or the traffic to chat about. Hiring managers have heard the same chatter from hundreds of different job hunters.

Instead, offer a compliment or a positive observation. You might mention how friendly everyone in the front office was to you, and give an example. You might compliment the handsome office and explain why you like it. Or, better yet, explain why you are so thrilled to be interviewing with this company. Make a good first impression and you'll set the tone for a good interview.

Another tip: If the hiring manager is escorting you to her office, ask for short tour to see the inner workings before the interview starts. Most people won't ask for a tour. If you do, the hiring manager will be impressed that you're interested—and that you asked. Plus, a short tour will give you a chance to establish a rapport with the hiring manager and gain an insight into her personality before the Q&A starts.

The start

Once you're both seated in the hiring manager's office, the manager will lean forward, smile and say, "Okay, tell me a little about yourself."

That's one of the most common opening questions. And, it's the perfect time to deliver your fifteen-second sales pitch from page 23. Your pitch is quick, to point, and it will show the hiring manager, right off, that you have the stuff she's looking for.

When you've finished delivering your pitch, offer the hiring manager your typed list of references. In return, ask for her business card. Asking for her business card is important—her business card will have all the information you'll need to follow-up after the interview is over.

The hiring manager will then take your resume out of her folder, give it a glance, and say, "I see here that you were the Over-and-Under guy at Round & Round. Can you tell me about your duties there?"

Keep in mind that your resume simply lists your accomplishments. It doesn't explain any

BECOME A STORY TELLER

Instead of explaining how or why you did something, try telling it as a story. Stories bring events to life.

A good story has three main parts, the beginning, middle, and end.

Another way to look at a good story is problem, struggle, outcome.

The problem, struggle, and outcome raise the energy of the story and make it more interesting.

Here's a little format you can use to craft your story.

- *Problem.* "I worked with some very difficult customers. For example..."
- *Struggle.* "I tried... I also tried... Then one day..."
- *Outcome.* "A week later..."

Keep your stories short and simple, about a minute each. Use your hands, facial expressions, and voice to bring them to life. Add a little humor whenever you can.

Stories can help you stand out. Long after you've left the interview, the hiring manager may not remember your name, but she'll remember your interesting story. "Hmmm," she'll think, "Maybe I should call that person who worked with all those difficult customers."

© COPYRIGHT, HARRY DAHLSTROM

of the back-story on those accomplishments. This is your chance to tell those stories. So, count off your main duties and tell how you turned each duty into an accomplishment. Be brief, but tell enough, and don't exaggerate—you don't need to.

The hiring manager will ask for details during your story. Give generous answers. Add a little humor when you can. Use hand gestures and facial expressions to bring your story to life.

If the conversation slows or lulls, weave in some questions of your own to create the ebb and flow of a two-way conversation. You might ask—

- "What are the department's goals for the year?"
- "What are the major challenges the new hire will face in this job?"
- "If hired, how long should it take for me to get my feet on the ground and become productive?"
- "Who are the key people I'd be working with and what do they do?"
- "Which employee do you rely upon most? What does she do and what makes her so reliable?"
- "How would I get feedback on my performance?"
- "How soon do you plan to fill this job?"

One thing, though, don't ask questions about wages, benefits, or vacations. To paraphrase President Kennedy, "Ask not what the company can do for you, show what you can do for the company." Besides, wages and benefits are usually discussed when the job offer is made.

The Q&A

By now you're probably warmed up and feeling a bit more confident. So, the hiring manager will start to ask some probing questions. She'll dig a little deeper into your work projects to measure your skills, personality, and judgment.

There are two types of questions the hiring manager will ask, common and behavioral. Common questions require a simple answer, "Can you work weekends?" Behavioral questions require some thought, "What would you do if one manager told you to do something and another manager told you not to do it?"

Hiring managers ask behavioral questions to see how you think, solve problems, and sort things out. There's usually no right or wrong answer.

There are fifty questions on pages 44 and 45 —both common and behavioral. There are also suggestions on how to answer them. Spend some time on those questions. Come up with a good answer for each one. You might write them down on flash cards and quiz yourself. You might also rehearse with a friend to get the kinks out of your answers, before the interview.

The close

Eventually, the conversation will start to slow down and the hiring manager will ask if you have any final questions. This is a sign that the interview is about to end.

Most of your questions will already be answered. But, you do want one or two solid, final questions up your sleeve. A good final question leaves a good final impression. Here are three:

- *You might ask a personal question.* "How did you get into the face-painting industry?" This shows that you're interested in other people and that you'll integrate easily into the team.

- *You could ask the manager to give you a thirty-day trial period to prove yourself.* It's a gutsy move that very few job hunters will offer, but it tells the hiring manager that you really want this job—and she'll remember that.

- *You could also ask, "How much autonomy or self-direction would I have on the job?"* This shows that you're responsible, a self-starter, the type of person who gets things done—a rare breed, a good catch.

When the hiring manager stands up, the interview is over. You should also stand. Then, look the hiring manager in the eye, smile, offer your handshake, and thank her for meeting with you.

Now, most job hunters never say whether they want the job or not, so make sure you do. You could simply say, "I'm pleased with what I've learned today. I want this position. Where do we go from here?"

The manager will probably say, "I'm still interviewing other candidates, I'll let you know."

Ask if you could follow up in a week, by phone, to see if she's made a decision

As she walks you to the door, say thanks again and mention that you hope she'll call.

And that's it.

Now, off to the follow-up on page 46.

SO, HOW'D YOU DO IN THERE?

Grade your interview with this easy scoring system:
❶ = Needs much more work
❷ = Just OK— room for improvement
❸ = Total win

Did you do your homework and know who the employer is, what they do, and why you want to work there?
❶　**❷**　**❸**

Did you know which skills were required for the job and show the manager that you are a good fit for that job?
❶　**❷**　**❸**

Did you offer examples to show that you are a hard worker and that you deliver more than the minimum?
❶　**❷**　**❸**

Did you answer tough questions without stumbling or getting flustered?
❶　**❷**　**❸**

Did you ask questions to learn more about the company and the job?
❶　**❷**　**❸**

Did you look the manager in the eye and speak clearly?
❶　**❷**　**❸**

Did you wear the proper clothes and look your best?
❶　**❷**　**❸**

Did you show enthusiasm, a sense of humor, and a positive attitude?
❶　**❷**　**❸**

Were you polite and respectful throughout the interview?
❶　**❷**　**❸**

Did you ask for the job?
❶　**❷**　**❸**

Add up your score. A perfect score is 30. Work on those areas where you need improvement. Think of every interview as practice for the next one.

© COPYRIGHT, HARRY DAHLSTROM

50 questions to expect during your job interview

1. "Can you tell me a little about yourself?"
Give your 15-second sales pitch from page 23. After you've given your sales pitch, hand the hiring manager a fresh copy of your resume plus your typed list of references. Next, this is important—ask for the hiring manager's business card. That business card will have all of the manager's contact information, including her email address and direct phone number. You'll need this information so you can stay in touch with the hiring manager after the interview is over.

2. "Tell me what you know about my company."
Before you go on the interview, be sure to visit the company's website. Get an overview of the company's key products and services. Google the company name for news. Find out who they are, what they do, and why you want to work for them.

3. "Why did you decide to become a snake charmer?"
Tell your story. Include lots of detail and use body language to bring your story to life. Add a touch of humor when appropriate.

4. "What skills or requirements do you think are needed for this job?"
Refer back to page 11. Use your fingers and count off the requirements: 1... 2... 3... 4... 5...

5. "What motivates you to do a good job?"
Money is not a good answer. Instead, try this: "Having responsibilities and getting a pat on the back when the job is done right."

6. "Why is customer service so important in business today?"
"Customers who receive helpful service from friendly employees are more apt to come back again and again. They are also more apt to tell their friends about us. Good service means more business."

7. "Why should I hire you instead of someone more qualified?"
Toot your horn. Tell the manager that you have more than good skills to offer— you're a team player, you're not afraid of hard work, you're a quick learner, you're reliable, you give more than just the minimum effort, and—you want to work for this company because...

8. "Did you ever have a disagreement with your boss?"
Answer "yes" and you're a troublemaker, answer "no" and you're a wimp. Find the middle ground: "Sure we disagreed. But we worked well together. For example..."

9. "Tell me about the toughest boss you ever worked

20. "What's your favorite book or movie? Why?"
Stay away from controversial issues.

21. "As a youngster, what did you do to earn your own spending money?"
Baby-sitting, lemonade stand, newspaper route, shoveling snow, mowing lawns, and other jobs show early signs of ambition and a respect for work.

22. "What do you do to relax after work?"
Don't brag about auto racing, bungee jumping, chain-saw juggling, or any other dangerous activity. They suggest a likelihood of injury and an absence from work. Instead, mention something wholesome like athletics, a hobby, a project, traveling, or entertaining friends.

23. "Are you at your best when working alone or in a group?"
"Both. I enjoy working as part of a team and I can work independently to get my share of the work done. For example..."

24. "Would you rather be in charge of a project or work as part of the team?"
"Either. I'm not afraid to take responsibility and I'm not afraid to roll up my sleeves and pitch in."

25. "Have you ever been fired from a job?"
Everybody gets fired from a job at least once in their lifetime. And don't be afraid to tell the truth if it was your fault. Fessing up says that you are a responsible, mature adult. Explain what happened. Explain what you learned. Explain what you would do differently if the same situation happened again.

26. "Tell me about your strengths."
From page 11, you know the five or six requirements needed for the job you want. Choose your strongest job requirements and offer examples to show how you excelled.

27. "What are your weaknesses?"
Choose one or two weaknesses that are not part of the job requirements. Be sure to include an action point to show what you did about each weakness. For instance, "I'm terrified of public speaking. I get so nervous I start to shake. So, I took a stand-up comedy class, online, to help get over the jitters and entertain my friends."

28. "Tell me about your favorite accomplishment."
A personal touch works well here, such as your marriage, birth of a child, or helping someone in need. You could also offer something both personal and benevolent. "I'm no athlete, but I did run a 5 kilometer road race in under 45 minutes—and I raised over $1,000 in pledges for

36. "If you were told to report to a supervisor who was a woman, a minority, or someone with a physical disability, what problems would this create for you?"
"I don't see any problems. I genuinely like people. I'm easy to coach and I'm easy to work with. For example..."

37. "Tell me, what would you do if one supervisor told you to do something, and another supervisor told you not to do it?"
The manager wants to see how you would handle a dilemma. Try this: Think about what would happen if you did act, and what would happen if you did not act. Write down the pros and cons of each. Make a decision.

38. "Tell me about a time when you broke the rules."
Sometimes it's necessary to break the rules. Just make sure your reasoning and judgement are sound.

39. "Can you tell me about a time when a supervisor was not pleased with your work?"
The manager wants to know how you react to criticism. Here are a few tips to keep in mind when preparing your answer: Top employees see criticism as a learning experience, not a reprimand. They listen without arguing or becoming defensive. They learn what needs to be done differently. They agree to the changes and implement them. They follow up by asking the supervisor for a critique of their new work. They also regain their enthusiasm and confidence quickly.

40. "Tell me about a time when you were swamped with work and how you handled it."
The manager wants to know how you prioritize your time. Experts suggest you start by making a list of all the tasks you need to do today. Next, arrange those tasks from most important to least important. Then, select the task which is most urgent. Start there.

41. "Please tell me about a time when you showed initiative at work."
Initiative is not about working harder. Initiative is about doing more than what your job requires. For example: Taking on a new responsibility without being asked, taking a class or reading a book to learn a new skill, or noticing a problem on the horizon and taking action to correct it.

42. "Describe a difficult decision you had to make."
The manager wants to know about your decision-making skills. Here's a basic decision-making formula: Define the problem, learn what others did in similar situations, list the pros and cons for each option, then choose the best option.

43. "Tell me about a time when you failed."

demanding, detail-driven perfectionist. But, I learned more from him than anyone I've ever worked with. For example…

10. "What salary or wage are you looking for?"
Get the manager to throw out the first figure. Ask, "What salary or wage do you usually offer someone with my skills and abilities?"

11. "Tell me about your current (or last) job."
Give the company's name and what they do. Give your job title. List your duties and responsibilities. Explain your accomplishments.

12. "Why are you leaving that job?"
Job stagnation, demotions due to downsizing, or simply having made a poor choice are all good reasons.

13. "What will your manager say when you give notice that you're leaving?"
Explain why you'll be missed. Don't give the impression that they'll be glad to be rid of you.

14. "Did you enjoy school?"
The manager wants to know if you enjoy learning and whether you might benefit from a training program.

15. "In school, which course did you find most difficult?"
The manager wants to know if you have perseverance: "My first term in history, I got a D. My study skills were all wrong, so I joined a study group. By second term I pulled it up to a B and kept it there."

16. Did you participate in any school activities?"
School activities show that you're sociable. They show that you enjoy being part of a group and that you can work with other people. This is important in the work place.

17. "Do you plan to continue your education?"
Adding to your education says that you want to grow and prosper, professionally as well as personally.

18. "What do you hope to get out of this job?"
Try this—"A reasonable paycheck, responsibility for doing something that matters, a say in how my work is done, recognition by my coworkers for being good at what I do, and, a pat on the back from the boss for doing a good job."

19. "Last year, how many days of work (or school) did you miss? How many days were you late?"
This will tell the manager whether you're going to show up for work on time every day. If you've missed more than a few days, have some good explanations ready.

and why did you choose them?"
"I chose a good mix—a former boss who can tell you about my skills and job performance—a coworker who can tell you about the hard work and extra effort we put in as a team—and a former coach who can tell you that I'm not only a good team player, I can work independently and I always complete my share of the work."

30. "What are the three things you look for when considering a new job?"
The things that make people happiest at work are not always about money and benefits. Experts say that the following things are often more important: being appreciated, having respect, being trusted, taking on new challenges, having a good boss, working with people you enjoy, and making a difference.

31. "How are you unique?"
Try this: "I'm a quick learner, a hard worker, I'm easy to coach, and I always deliver more than what's expected. I could be one of the best employees you'll ever hire."

▶ The following include some behavioral questions. Behavioral questions help the manager see how you might act or behave in certain situations.

32. "Tell me how you keep a positive attitude when the job gets stressful?"
Here's how positive people stay positive: They know that attitude is a choice. They choose to plan ahead and schedule the time needed to get things done. They choose to be around other positive people. They choose to laugh and have a sense of humor. They choose to be friendly and helpful to everyone. They choose to offset negative thoughts by looking for the positive points.

33. "Please tell me about a time when you had to motivate a coworker."
Some of the best motivational tools include praise and encouragement, giving a helpful demonstration or example, explaining the rewards of the job, and brainstorming for better ways to do the job.

34. "Can you tell me about a goal you set for yourself?"
The manager wants to know if you set goals. People who set goals are more productive than those who do not set goals. The best goals are specific, measurable, and plausible. For example, "I want to pay off my $1,000 car loan in six months," is a better goal than, "I want to pay off my car loan quickly."

35. "Describe a problem you faced and how you solved that problem."
Think of something related to work, school, sports, or volunteering. Tell it as a story. The manager wants to see how you: 1) Define the problem, 2) Identify options and, 3) Decide on a solution.

44. "Describe a time when you had to work with a difficult person."
The manager wants to see how you interact with moody, lazy, or obnoxious people. Ideally, you are a peacemaker who tries to resolve conflicts. When provoked, you have a private talk with the person. You remain pleasant. You explain how the behavior makes you feel. And you try to reach an agreement with the culprit.

45. "Please tell me about a time when you were disappointed."
The manager isn't so much interested in what happened, but what you did about that disappointment. Try something like this. "When I didn't get the promotion—I was surprised and hurt. But, I swallowed my pride and congratulated the winner—she earned that promotion. The next day, I reviewed my work performance. I redoubled my efforts, and I haven't missed a promotion since."

46. "Tell me about a project you worked on."
The manager wants to know about your role in the project, specifically what you did. Begin by describing the project and the project's goal. Then, describe the team you worked with, specifically your duties, your responsibilities, your contribution, and any new skills you learned. Finally, tell whether the project met its goals.

47. "Tell me where you expect to be 5 years from now?"
Try this: "It's hard to know where anyone will be five years from now. But, I am looking for a company where I'll be appreciated, trusted, and able to make a difference. I want to work with people I enjoy, people who challenge me, and a good boss who's not afraid to tell us we did a good job. I think your company might be the one I'm looking for. That's why I'm here today."

48. "Are there any questions I didn't ask, that I should have asked?"
This is a great time to bring up any special skill, ability, or accomplishment that wasn't discussed.

49. "Okay, you've got one minute to convince me that you're the best person for this job. Begin."
Do it in only 30 seconds and you'll make a big impression. Start by delivering your 15-second sales pitch. Then, spend 15 seconds explaining why you want to work for this company. End by asking for the job.

50. "Do you have any questions for me?"
On page 42, you'll find a list of questions to ask the hiring manager. Add a few questions of your own to the list.

The Job Hunting Handbook, © Copyright, Harry Dahlstrom

The art of the follow-up

When you get home from your interview, send the manager a thank-you note. Two days later, send the manager an *idea* note. A week after your interview, pick up the phone and give the manager a call. Then, stay in touch with that hiring manager.

1. Send a thank-you note

Most job hunters do send thank-you notes. You should send them too.

Keep in mind that businesses are formal. Manners are important. Thank-you notes are expected. Managers look for these things.

Keep your thank-you note brief.

- Thank the manager for meeting with you and mention the date and job title you interviewed for.
- Say that you want the job.
- Give one or two solid reasons why the hiring manager should offer you the job.
- Offer the manager a thirty-day trial period to prove yourself.
- Say that you'd like to call in a week or so to see if she's made a decision.

Write your thank-you note and send it off within 24 hours of the interview so the manager will remember who you are.

2. Send an idea note

Now, here's something hardly any of your competitors will try—

During your interview, the manager asked if you had any questions for her. You said, "Yes, what are the major challenges the new hire will face in this job?"

Now, think about the manager's answer. If the problems are not confidential, discuss them with a friend or look for a solution online. Come up with a few suggestions. Then, send

55%

Fifty-five percent of job hunters send thank-you notes to the people who interviewed them.

—Vault.com

the manager a short note explaining your ideas.

Your suggestions don't have to be brilliant, just good. The point is, the manager will see that you're a problem solver and that you were the only one who made an extra effort to win the job offer.

Send your idea note a day or so after your thank-you note, but before you follow-up on the telephone.

3. Call the manager

A week after your interview, call the manager to see if she's made a decision. Yes, everybody hates making these calls. But, it shows that you're the kind of person who gets things done—even if the task is unpleasant. Use the calling script on the right.

4. If you didn't get the job, stay in touch

Once or twice a month, send every hiring manager who interviewed you a short note and another copy of your resume. Let them know that you are still available and that you are still interested in working for them.

Remember, jobs open up all the time. Some people decline job offers. Some change their minds and quit. Other people don't work out and management lets them go.

Sometimes jobs also open up in other departments as well. Most managers are eager to refer solid applicants to other hiring managers.

So, stay in touch with all your hiring managers. They are your inside connection—and a gentle persistence can re-open doors. The idea is to become the first person they think of when something new opens up.

—Best wishes, Harry Dahlstrom

CALL THE HIRING MANAGER AND SEE IF YOU GOT THE JOB

Call the manager and introduce yourself.
"Good morning, Ms. Hireyou. This is Emma Gogetter. I wanted to call and thank you for meeting with me last week about your lion tamer's position."

Ask if the manager has made a decision.
"I'm very interested in that position and I thought I might follow-up to see if you've made a decision."

If you got the job—
"Really? Yikes! Hey Ma..."

"When would you like me to start?"

"What time should I report?"

"Where should I report?"

"To whom should I report?"

"What do I need to bring with me on the first day?"

If the manager hasn't yet made a decision—
"Am I still a candidate for consideration?"

"I'd love to have this job. Would you consider giving me a trial period to prove myself?"

If she needs time to think it over, ask—"Would it be okay if I call back on Friday?"

If you didn't get the job—
Don't beg, don't lose your cool, and don't close any doors. You might say—

"Gee, I'm sorry to hear that."

"Ms. Hireyou, I'd like to thank you for your time and consideration. It was a pleasure to meet you and to learn about your company."

"If the person you chose for this job becomes unavailable, please call me. I'd be happy to come in for another interview."

Then, keep in mind that you've been reaching out to 5 new employers every day. That's 25 employers a week and 100 a month. A lot more interviews and job offers are coming your way.

© COPYRIGHT, HARRY DAHLSTROM

CPSIA information can be obtained
at www.ICGtesting.com
Printed in the USA
BVHW011751020322
630441BV00005B/89